D1281867

LITERARY CONVI

LITERARY CONVERTS

SPIRITUAL INSPIRATION IN
AN AGE OF UNBELIEF

JOSEPH PEARCE

HarperCollins*Publishers*

HarperCollins*Religious*
Part of HarperCollins*Publishers*
77–85 Fulham Palace Road, London W6 8JB
www.christian-publishing.com

First published in Great Britain in 1999 by HarperCollins*Religious*

© 1999 Joseph Pearce

1 2 3 4 5 6 7 8 9 10

Joseph Pearce asserts the moral right to be identified as the author of this work

A catalogue record for this book is available from the British Library

ISBN 0 00 628111 7

Printed and bound in Great Britain by
Creative Print and Design (Wales), Ebbw Vale